S'MOREGASBORD

101 NOVEL S'MORE RECIPES TO TRY

JULIE BICKEL
ALENA VAN ARENDONK
LAURA VAN ARENDONK BAUGH

AECLIPSE PRESS
INDIANAPOLIS

CONTENTS

INTRODUCTION

Thousands of years ago, the sap of the marshmallow plant was blended with honey and grain and baked into cakes for ancient Egyptian nobility. As millennia passed, marshmallow remained a vegetable and a medical treatment (an anti–inflammatory and laxative) prescribed by Greek, Roman, and Arab physicians for everything from the common cold to toothache. It wasn't until the 19th century that French candymakers began to whip marshmallow root with egg white and sugar or syrup to produce a moldable sweet, called *pâté de guimauve*. (I speak no French, but Julie assures me this translates as "tasty lanyard[1]," as they were prepared in long ropes.) Once the result was marketed as a treat instead of as medicine, the marshmallow component itself was replaced with gelatin or gum arabic, though the name remained.

Chocolate also has an ancient history but a much different modernization. It was first served as a fermented beverage, at least by 1000 BCE but possibly a thousand years before. European colonization brought the New World crop and by the 17th century chocolate houses were popular in the way that coffee houses are today. Then in 1875 the first solid milk chocolate was produced, and the way was paved for modern indulging.

The graham cracker was famously invented by Sylvester Graham in the early 19th century as an aid to reducing sexual obsession and greed, vices which he thought were fueled by indulgent foods. After his passing, the National Biscuit Company (now Nabisco) sweetened the cracker, to Graham's probable posthumous disapproval, to arrive at today's popular snack.

By the 1920s the sacred trio of graham cracker, marshmallow, and chocolate in sandwich form had been realized, though not yet with its iconic moniker. In 1927 the Girl Scouts, those intrepid inventors, published the simple recipe in their handbook *Tramping and Trailing With The Girl Scouts*, with the first known dubbing of "Some More."

Modern marshmallows have given up any pretense of medicinal value, but they have fixed themselves into campfire culture as a favorite rustic—and now upscale—treat.

When Laura and Alena were children, their father told a campfire story of how Charlie Chunk'o'chocolate, Mighty Marshmallow, and Andy Grahamcracker went on an adventure, fell off a cliff, and tumbled together into a squishy pile, a frightening escapade which turned out to be so surprisingly fun that they wanted to do it s'more! We invite you to bring this giddy sense of experimental joy to this collection.

It's important to note that s'mores began as a simple, rustic treat. While some of our creations may appear more complex or even snooty, the result should always be fun, or we have failed. All can be eaten with fingers

---

[1] Okay, okay. The ropey shape is true. But *guimauve* is the French name of the plant.

(though some will require more cleanup than others, and if you are preparing treats for small hands you may want to stick to the All Ages chapter for less mess), and every one of these s'mores was created outdoors over a wood fire—no gourmet kitchen or specialized tools needed. Long live the s'more.

A NOTE ON INGREDIENTS

We experimented with a wide variety of crackers, cookies, marshmallows, and toppings. In some cases, we have noted where a specific brand or type makes enough of a difference to matter. Most of the time, it doesn't. But here are our expert opinions to consider as you make out your shopping list.

❖ The vegan marshmallows we tried were better than the more common variety for eating plain and untoasted, with a better texture and flavor, but they did not roast as well. However, for vegan, kosher, halal, and other diet considerations, they are an acceptable alternative.

❖ The specially–sized and squared off "for s'mores" marshmallows were in fact less useful for general purposes, being too dense to heat evenly through without more care than hungry chefs are willing to expend. We have included them in some recipes for the higher load of marshmallow, but you may be happier with the regular model.

❖ Homemade more traditional marshmallows, made with honey and real marshmallow (remember, these started as medicine!), are delicious but do not roast well at all; honey melts!

❖ While any decent chocolate bar will serve, choices can make a difference, so feel free to experiment. And if you really want to feel good about your snacking, consider buying fair trade or organic chocolate, both made without the child and slave labor usually contributing to the mainstream chocolate supply. While chocolate manufacturers have repeatedly promised to be more ethical in their sourcing, the reality is cost matters more and bulk purchases make it easy to hide brutal practices. The paper trail required for fair trade and organic certification make such exploitation much more difficult.

❖ There are many recipes for toffee saltines, fundamentally brown sugar and butter baked into caramel atop a saltine cracker (also known as a soda cracker). Most are simple; use any that strikes your fancy! Ours includes chocolate atop the toffee. Just remember not to use salted butter if you're using a salted cracker.

HOW TO TOAST THE PERFECT MARSHMALLOW

The debate over what constitutes a properly toasted marshmallow has caused nearly as many family rifts as the board game *Monopoly*. Some connoisseurs aim for a smooth golden finish, while others prefer their 'mallows wreathed in flame and cocooned inside a crackling black crust.

We are not here to settle this hotly contested issue. Whether you like your marshmallows barely warmed or carbonized and flaking, we encourage you to customize this sweet treat to your own taste.

We *will*, however, tell you how to prepare marshmallows suitable for making the perfect s'more. Unlike marshmallows eaten *à la carte*, s'mores require the marshmallow to be warmed through the center, so it is soft enough to flatten between the crackers and retains enough heat to melt the chocolate. If the marshmallow is heated too quickly, the center will remain cool and solid while the outside will become too dry. (Sorry, torch–wielding marshmallow roasters; setting your 'mallow on fire doesn't heat it evenly.)

The key to even heating is to keep your marshmallow near the glowing embers at the base of the fire, rather than the open flames at the top. The radiant heat from the coals will surround the marshmallow without instantly catching it on fire. It's also important to rotate your marshmallow frequently so that the outer surface toasts evenly. (If you are using a metal roasting fork, keep it as level as possible so the marshmallow does not melt around the hot metal and slide off the tines.)

When the marshmallow has puffed up to about 150% of its original size and the outer surface is turning a light golden brown, it is ready to be smashed between layers of s'more ingredients.

TRADITIONAL & SIMPLE S'MORES

THE CLASSIC

plain graham cracker
milk chocolate
plain marshmallow

A BIT DARKER

plain graham cracker
dark chocolate
plain marshmallow

THE COMMITTED CHOCOLATIER

Substitute a chocolate graham cracker in either.

We should start with the iconic foundation of all s'mores. While the rest of this book is devoted to variations on this theme, in no way do we suggest that this classic is inferior on its own.

This hinges on a perfectly roasted marshmallow. Take your time.

STRAWBERRY 'MALLOW

plain graham cracker
dark chocolate
strawberry marshmallow

DARK STRAWBERRY 'MALLOW

chocolate graham cracker
dark chocolate
strawberry marshmallow

MOAR STRAWBERRY

chocolate graham cracker
dark chocolate
strawberry marshmallow
strawberry

The strawberry marshmallows taste best this way! The dark chocolate offsets the artificial flavoring.

JAM S'MOOKIE

chocolate sandwich cookies
milk chocolate
plain marshmallow
cherry preserves

A little fruit can lighten the texture and brighten the overall taste of a sugary s'more. You don't need a sweetened jam; there's plenty of sugar already. Let the fruit shine.

YOU GOT PEANUT BUTTER IN MY S'MORE

plain graham cracker
Reese's Thins Peanut Butter Cup
plain marshmallow

This is a ridiculously simple swap in a basic s'more and yet adds a whole additional dimension of flavor with the saltiness of the peanut butter.

MORE 'MALLOW & CHOCOLATE MORE 'MALLOW

plain or chocolate graham cracker
milk chocolate
Kraft Jet Puffed S'moreMallows

As mentioned before, the larger S'moreMallows are more difficult to perfectly toast—but if you are a marshmallow lover above all else, you can find a denser marshmallow here. (Or you can simply roast two ordinary marshmallows at once.)

the common

marsh mallow

HAZELNUT COOKIE 1

chocolate sandwich cookies
milk chocolate
plain marshmallow
hazelnut spread

HAZELNUT COOKIE 2

chocolate sandwich cookies
milk chocolate
plain marshmallow
hazelnut spread
raspberries
chocolate balsamic vinegar

SIMPLE SPREAD 1

plain graham cracker
plain marshmallow
cream cheese
chocolate chips

SIMPLE SPREAD 2

chocolate graham cracker
plain marshmallow
hazelnut spread
chocolate chips
raspberries

MEAT & POTATOES

Ruffles Original potato chip
milk chocolate
plain marshmallow
bacon

CHOCOLATE-DIPPED POTATO

chocolate-dipped Ruffles Original potato chip
plain marshmallow
bacon

You'd think this would crumble, but melty 'mallow holds it together as you eat. This is another tasty variation for the salty-snacks fan who worries s'mores are too sweet. Dipping the potato chips is a fun activity for kids and produces a striking aesthetic.

CHOCOLATE-DIPPED BACON S'MORE

Ruffles Original potato chip
plain marshmallow
chocolate—covered bacon

This is the best of the potato chip variants. The blend of salty and sweet is most balanced here, and the texture of the chocolate—dipped bacon is a welcome contrast to the gooey s'more.

S'MORES FOR ALL AGES

BANANA CHOCOLATE

chocolate graham cracker
plain marshmallow
chocolate covered banana slice

Bananas are easy to dip in melted chocolate chips and are a great way to sneak more fruits into your dessert.

MARSHMALLOW COOKIE

OREO Double Stuf Cookies
milk chocolate
Kraft Jet Puffed S'moreMallows

This one is for the marshmallow lovers.

The extra crème filling and the oversized S'moreMallow make for a very creamy experience. As mentioned, take some extra time to roast your larger S'moreMallow carefully. A perfect marshmallow explosion of crisp outer shell and warm, soft middle is worth it.

CHOCOLATE CHOCOLATE BANANA

chocolate graham cracker
milk chocolate
plain marshmallow
chocolate–dipped banana

Bananas and chocolate go together surprisingly well, and no one seems to appreciate that quite as much as they should.

BANANA PEANUT CHOCOLATE

chocolate graham cracker
Reese's Thins Peanut Butter Cup
plain marshmallow
plain banana

BANANA CHOCOLATE COOKIE

OREO Double Stuf sandwich cookies
dark chocolate
plain marshmallow
chocolate–dipped banana

TOFFEE

toffee cracker
plain marshmallow

BACON S'MORE

plain graham cracker
milk chocolate
plain marshmallow
bacon bits

Banana slices, chocolate pieces, and crackers and cookies are easy building blocks for small fingers. Set out a variety of components and let kids choose and assemble their own.

BANANA CHOCOLATE CHIP

chocolate chip cookies
milk chocolate
plain marshmallow
chocolate-drizzled banana

"I never knew banana would be so amazing on a s'more."

Homemade chocolate chip cookies make excellent foundations for s'mores of many varieties.

SHORTBREAD ELVIS

shortbread
dark chocolate
plain marshmallow
banana, peanut butter

CHOCOLATE BANANA SHORTBREAD

shortbread
dark chocolate
plain marshmallow
chocolate–dipped banana, peanut butter

This one is particularly tasty for shortbread lovers. Typical shortbread cookies may be a bit thick for this, so either find or make some thin ones or relish the extra shortbread texture.

CHOCOLATE ELVIS

chocolate graham cracker
plain marshmallow
chocolate–dipped banana, peanut butter, whipped
cream

I mean, look at this. You just can't help falling in love with it. One bite, and you'll be all shook up. If you're lonesome tonight, don't be cruel to yourself: make one of these.

PEANUT BUTTER STUFFED COOKIE

OREO Double Stuf Sandwich Cookies
Reese's Thins Peanut Butter Cup
vanilla marshmallow

This is so simple and so good.

While it's hard to go too wrong with a peanut butter cup, we recommend the Reese's Thins for a s'more–optimal blend and size.

STRAWBERRY MINT

mint chocolate sandwich cookies
dark chocolate
strawberry marshmallow

Our tester thought this combination of flavored components was a bit artificial, but that flavor extreme is exactly what some kids delight in (have you seen their breakfast cereals?) and that's why it's here for them. We have plenty of other s'mores for the grownups.

CHOCOLATE COOKIE

chocolate sandwich cookies
milk chocolate
plain marshmallow

A very simple variation, but one with a considerable difference in s'more experience.

CHOCOLATE PEANUT BUTTER CUP

chocolate sandwich cookie
Reese's Thins Peanut Butter Cup
plain marshmallow

No, this is not a responsible adult choice. Not even close. But you are an adult and so you can choose to do it anyway, because no one else is the boss of you.

CHOCOLATE CHIPPER

chocolate chip cookies
milk chocolate
plain marshmallow

THE MOSTEST 'MALLOW

chocolate sandwich cookies
milk chocolate
Kraft Jet Puffed S'moreMallows

THE MOSTEST 'MALLOW 2

mint chocolate sandwich cookies
milk chocolate
Kraft Jet Puffed S'moreMallows

There are nearly infinite possibilities for combining your favorite cookies with traditional s'more ingredients. Customize to your favorite combination of homemade and storebought treats, of gooey soft chocolate chip cookies or crunchy sandwich cookies, or something completely different.

COOKIES & STRAWBERRY

chocolate sandwich cookies
milk chocolate
strawberry marshmallow

We found flavored marshmallows could have a chalky taste out of the bag, but toasting them thoroughly helped to diminish that in the final s'more. Roast well.

LUCKY KIDS

plain graham cracker
milk chocolate
Kraft Lucky Charms Marshmallows

LUCKY KIDS 2

chocolate graham cracker
milk chocolate
Kraft Lucky Charms Marshmallows

LUCKY STUFF

OREO Double Stuf Sandwich Cookies
milk chocolate
Kraft Lucky Charms Marshmallows

Add a pop of color with these branded marshmallows, but be aware their shapes (vague to begin with) will not survive toasting.

These colorful marshmallows are small, so they toast quickly (great for impatient little s'more chefs) but can burn easily (not so great for beginners). Stay close to lend a hand.

CINNAMON ROLL

cinnamon graham cracker
vanilla marshmallow
cream cheese

A s'more without chocolate? I know, but we don't think you'll regret trying it. Think of your favorite cinnamon roll (breakfast food or fictional character) while preparing it.

THE MINT SANDWICH

mint chocolate sandwich cookies
milk chocolate
plain marshmallow

THE VANILLA MINT SANDWICH

mint chocolate sandwich cookies
milk chocolate
vanilla marshmallow

Plenty of cream, with a bit of mint to keep it from being overwhelming.

BROWN BUTTER S'MORE

plain graham cracker
brown butter chocolate
plain marshmallow
caramel

This might look like an ordinary s'more from the outside, but the complexity of flavors makes it a secret delight.

S'MORES FOR THE DISCERNING PALATE

BLUEBERRY BALSAMIC

plain graham cracker
dark chocolate
plain marshmallow
blueberry Stilton cheese
chocolate balsamic vinegar

This was one of the first Stilton s'mores we tried and it immediately leveled the iconic treat to a Grown–Up Dessert. The balsamic vinegar makes a real difference, too.

BLUEBERRY MAPLE

LU Pétit Écolier cookies
plain marshmallow
blueberry Stilton cheese, whipped cream,
maple syrup

BLUEBERRY MAPLE BACON

add bacon bits

Whatever has gone wrong with your day, this can
probably fix it. The sweet cheese and salty bacon,
all under maple, are a winning combination.

SPICED CHERRY CHEESECAKE

plain graham cracker
milk chocolate
plain marshmallow
spiced cherry preserves, cream cheese

Deceptively simple. An easy upgrade to the classic s'more.

CHOCOLATE BALSAMIC

LU Pétit Écolier cookies
plain marshmallow
chocolate balsamic vinegar

This is a place where a good balsamic vinegar can shine. Feel free to experiment with whatever flavors you may have.

CINNAMON FIRE

cinnamon graham cracker
milk chocolate
plain marshmallow
whiskey–drizzled marshmallow
sprinkle of cinnamon

BLUEBERRY BOOZE

plain graham cracker
dark chocolate
plain marshmallow
brandy–drizzled marshmallow
blueberry pomegranate preserves

A S'MORE FOR ADULTS, SORRY

LU Pétit Écolier cookies
plain marshmallow
brandy–drizzled marshmallow

STRAWBERRY BALSAMIC

LU Pétit Écolier cookies
plain marshmallow
strawberry balsamic vinegar

RASPBERRY STUFFING

OREO Double Stuf Sandwich Cookies
plain marshmallow
raspberries

You may see whiskey as an ingredient and be tempted, as we were, to attempt to flambé a marshmallow to create a slightly boozy and self–toasting s'more.

This is a better idea in concept than in execution.

In traditional cookery, the alcohol is heated beforehand to help its combustion. A cool evening, while perfect for marshmallow toasting, is not an ideal temperature to spark alcohol which is difficult to light at room temperature. And we cannot in good conscience recommend the warming of combustible alcohol with open flame, such as your roasting fire.

Therefore, we must recommend against the attempt to flambé a s'more in typical circumstances. You are more likely to melt your marshmallow in a disappointing display of physics than to successfully flame your whiskey or brandy. You may, however, drizzle or soak, and we won't tell.

CHERRY BERRY

plain graham cracker
dark chocolate
vanilla marshmallow
spiced cherry preserves
strawberries

DARK & FRUITY

chocolate graham cracker
dark chocolate
vanilla marshmallow
spiced cherry preserves
strawberries

Our tester noted that the chocolate graham cracker was superior in flavor, and that the strawberries matter here.

CINNAMON CHEESECAKE

cinnamon graham cracker
milk chocolate
plain marshmallow
cream cheese
strawberry

A schmear of cream cheese on each cinnamon−y cracker and sliced strawberries lend a bit of urban sophistication to this rustic icon.

CHERRY TOFFEE

toffee cracker
dark chocolate
plain marshmallow
spiced cherry preserves

A cracker upgrade and a single addition to the basic s'more yields this striking entry. Go ahead and lick your fingers.

CHOCOLATE CHEESECAKE

chocolate graham cracker
chocolate chips
plain marshmallow
cream cheese

It's cream cheese, not ricotta, but if you close your eyes and pretend, it's almost like eating a cannoli. If you'd set the cannoli on fire.

SPICED CHERRY

plain graham cracker
dark chocolate
vanilla marshmallow
spiced cherry preserves

BERRY BERRY

plain graham cracker
dark chocolate
plain marshmallow
blueberry pomegranate preserves
raspberries

CHOCOLATE MAPLE BACON

plain graham cracker
milk chocolate
plain marshmallow
bacon bits
bourbon maple bacon balsamic vinegar

CHOCOLATE & CREAM CHEESE

chocolate graham cracker
chocolate chips
plain marshmallow
cream cheese
chocolate balsamic vinegar

HAZELNUT

chocolate graham cracker
cinnamon graham cracker
chocolate chips
plain marshmallow
hazelnut spread

CREAMY JALAPEÑO

plain graham cracker
milk chocolate
plain marshmallow
cream cheese
jalapeño jelly

SPICY SCHOOLBOY

LU Pétit Écolier cookies
dark chocolate
plain marshmallow
spiced cherry preserves

SALTY SCHOOLBOY

LU Pétit Écolier cookies
plain marshmallow
cream cheese
bacon bits

MAPLE BACON

LU Pétit Écolier cookies
plain marshmallow
bourbon maple balsamic vinegar, bacon bits

The maple is a nice flavor in this one,
complementing the bacon.

STILTON MAPLE WHIP

plain graham cracker
milk chocolate
plain marshmallow
blueberry Stilton cheese, maple syrup,
whipped cream, bacon bits

Use just a tiny bit of maple syrup here to finish it.
The whipped cream gives a bit of polish.

FRUIT & CHEESE PLATTER

plain graham cracker
dark chocolate
plain marshmallow
blueberry Stilton cheese, strawberries, strawberry
balsamic vinegar

A rich blend of fruit and cheese flavors. This is a
very sophisticated s'more. Feel free to extend your
pinky as you nom.

DECADENT BREAKFAST S'MORE

LU Pétit Écolier cookies
plain marshmallow
cream cheese, bacon bits, maple syrup

Sweet and sticky with the syrup, exactly like a weekend breakfast should be. Use real maple syrup for best flavor.

COCONUT MELT

LU Pétit Écolier cookies
plain marshmallow
toasted coconut, melted chocolate drizzle

DECADENT COCONUT MELT

Add whipped cream and maraschino cherry .

Having guests over? These can be simple and stunning upgrades to a classic cookout dessert.

Because these cookies are firmer than graham crackers, you can get a really strong contrast between firm chocolate and melty marshmallow.

ANTIOXIDANT SPECIAL

LU Pétit Écolier cookies
dark chocolate
plain marshmallow
blueberry pomegranate preserves

Dark chocolate, blueberries, pomegranate—this is a trove of healthy antioxidant goodness. The marshmallow just helps it to go down smoothly, that's all. Tell your doctor I said so.

CHOCOLATE & FRUIT

chocolate graham cracker
dark chocolate
plain marshmallow
blueberry pomegranate preserves, raspberries

Julie liked this—a lot. She reports, "Raspberries make it amazing. If you hate happiness, you may omit the raspberries."

BANANA SPLIT

chocolate graham cracker
plain marshmallow
chocolate covered banana slice, walnuts, whipped
cream, chocolate drizzle

Whipped cream is an important addition here. We're not talking about that fluffed up oil stuff—go for the real dairy product. You're having dessert. (And it's better for you.)

SUPER SUNDAE S'MORE

plain graham cracker
milk chocolate
vanilla marshmallow
maraschino cherry, whipped cream, walnuts, melted
chocolate drizzle

The vanilla marshmallow allows you to have a
warm sundae that still melts in your mouth. Enjoy
at any time of year.

TOFFEE & BACON

toffee cracker
plain marshmallow
bacon bits

What if we could get many complementary flavors into as few pieces as possible while keeping the resulting s'more finger−friendly? Oh yeah.

BRUNCH S'MORE

shortbread
dark chocolate
plain marshmallow
blueberry Stilton cheese, whipped cream,
maple syrup, bacon bits

Take "brunch on the patio" to a whole new level
with this bite−sized breakfast treat. Mmm.

BLUEBERRY DREAM

plain graham cracker
milk chocolate
plain marshmallow
blueberry Stilton cheese
blueberry pomegranate preserves

This is amazing. The Stilton adds just a hint of savor, while its blueberry melds with the preserves. The result goes together surprisingly well with marshmallow and chocolate.

CHOCOLATE MINT

chocolate graham cracker
dark chocolate
plain marshmallow
chocolate–dipped mint leaf

Simple and delicious.

Use ordinary chocolate chips for melting and dipping; they're much better than candy melts.

PUT THE MALLOW IN THE COCONUT

plain graham cracker
coconut white chocolate
plain marshmallow
roll marshmallow in (optionally toasted) coconut
shavings

You can either squeeze the marshmallow a bit and
use the gooey middle to adhere the shaved coconut,
or you can coat the marshmallow in melted
chocolate and roll it. Both ways are fun and tasty.

HAZELNUT RASPBERRY

plain graham cracker
dark chocolate
vanilla marshmallow
hazelnut spread
raspberries

HAZELNUT STRAWBERRY

plain graham cracker
dark chocolate
vanilla marshmallow
hazelnut spread
strawberries

Berries add a juicy pop of natural sweetness and a contrasting texture. This is a great place to introduce raspberries to picky eaters or to indulge in that fresh produce sale you found.

MINT RASPBERRY

plain graham cracker
dark chocolate
plain marshmallow
raspberries, mint leaf

Raspberries add a combination of sweet and tart that pairs well with the mint, the dark chocolate, and the sugary marshmallow.

SUNDAE S'MORE

shortbread
milk chocolate
plain marshmallow
melted chocolate, coconut, cherry,
whipped cream

Deliciously fluffy marshmallow on firm shortbread with your favorite sundae toppings. Add walnuts or another nut if desired.

ANTIOXIDANT SPECIAL 2

chocolate graham cracker
dark chocolate
vanilla marshmallow
blueberry pomegranate preserves

CHERRY CHOCOLATE

chocolate graham cracker
dark chocolate
vanilla marshmallow
spiced cherry preserves

CHOCOLATE BLUEBERRY

plain graham cracker
dark chocolate
vanilla marshmallow
blueberry pomegranate preserves

CHIPS & CREAM

chocolate and cinnamon graham crackers
chocolate chips
plain marshmallow
cream cheese

REFINED S'MORE

plain graham cracker
milk chocolate
plain marshmallow
blueberry Stilton cheese
raspberries

We liked this decadent entry quite a lot. This is the s'more to bring out when someone says s'mores are too messy and too juvenile. The Stilton cheese and the raspberries are anything but juvenile, while the chocolate and marshmallow keep a sense of fun.

SEASONAL S'MORES

PUMPKIN PIE

shortbread
white chocolate
plain marshmallow
pumpkin pie filling, cloves, allspice, nutmeg,
ginger, cinnamon, whipped cream

Worth going over the river and through the woods for, this bite-sized pumpkin pie can be customized to your spice preferences. We liked ours flavorful!

GINGERSNAP SLIDERS

gingersnap
white chocolate
plain marshmallow
cream cheese frosting, cinnamon

Tiny and tasty, these provide some zing among your sweet lineup.

CARAMEL LATTE

cinnamon graham cracker
white chocolate
plain marshmallow
caramel, whipped cream, instant coffee

Sprinkle the instant coffee inside to taste and on top for aesthetic. Because aesthetic mattters, too.

STRAWBERRY SHORTBREAD

shortbread
milk chocolate
plain marshmallow
cream cheese
strawberry balsamic vinegar

STRAWBERRY SHORTBREAD JAMMY

shortbread
dark chocolate
plain marshmallow
strawberry jam

CREAMY STRAWBERRY SHORTBREAD

shortbread
dark chocolate
plain marshmallow
strawberry jam
cream cheese

These small shortbread cookies make an admirable base for s'more "sliders" to experiment with different combinations without committing to a full-sized s'more. Mix and match until you find your favorite.

PUMPKIN SPICE LATTE

cinnamon graham cracker
white chocolate
plain marshmallow
pumpkin pie filling, cloves, allspice, nutmeg,
ginger, cinnamon, instant coffee,
whipped cream

With traditional pumpkin spices, a dollop of healthy pumpkin, and a shot of ground energy sprinkled over the top, you can justify this s'more in any of several ways.

S'MORES TO SHOW OFF

SALTED CARAMEL

plain graham cracker
milk chocolate
plain marshmallow
caramel, coarse salt

As mentioned with the Apple Pie s'mores, a good caramel makes a difference here. The salty–sweet contrast is justly popular. Enjoy!

DANGEROUS

chocolate graham cracker
dark chocolate
plain marshmallow
cinnamon graham cracker
spiced cherry preserves
marshmallow
toffee cracker
bourbon bacon balsamic vinegar
chocolate balsamic vinegar
bacon bits

THE NAKED DANGEROUS

chocolate graham cracker
milk chocolate
plain marshmallow
cinnamon graham cracker
spiced cherry preserves
marshmallow
toffee cracker

A decadent s'more for special occasions. Layering makes each flavor and texture stand apart for a more complex s'more dining experience.

MEMENTO MORI-O

OREO chocolate sandwich cookies
dark chocolate
plain marshmallow
hazelnut spread
chocolate balsamic vinegar
whipped cream

Julie tripped on equipment during this photoshoot and reported, "I was staging the Memento Mori−o and I kicked the bucket!"

Not only is this a great flavor combination, it's an immensely fun s'more for a theme party. Play it up for classic Hallowe'en events.

CARAMEL APPLE

cinnamon graham cracker
plain marshmallow
caramel, apple slice, chocolate drizzle

Our tester: "I went to my knees and made noises like an elephant in love." A bit dramatic, maybe, but this one is very, very good.

CARAMEL APPLE 2

cinnamon graham cracker
plain marshmallow
caramel, apple slices, chocolate drizzle, chopped nuts

An autumn classic. We used walnuts, but adapt as desired.

APPLE PIE

cinnamon graham cracker
plain marshmallow
caramel
apple slice
apple butter
cinnamon
whipped cream

APPLE PIE 2

shortbread
plain marshmallow
caramel
apple slice
apple butter
cinnamon
whipped cream

For these and for the Caramel Apple s'mores, the caramel makes a real difference. We used a local specialty, DeBrand Buttery Caramel, but you may use any good caramel. Just don't cheat yourself with a "caramel flavor" syrup in a plastic bottle. Buy something good or make it yourself (it's not hard!) and then enjoy the results.

THE INDEPENDENCE

plain graham cracker
milk chocolate
plain marshmallow
cherry preserves, blue icing, star sprinkles,
star pick with maraschino cherry

This colorful celebration includes cherry jam to honor that cherry tree George Washington didn't actually chop down but we talk about anyway. Sprinkles make it fun for kids (and adults) to assemble.

TURTLES ALL THE WAY

chocolate graham cracker
milk chocolate
plain marshmallow
caramel, chopped pecans

The classic turtle, now in s'more form. Delicious.

THE DAGWOOD

In order:

plain graham cracker (full)
milk chocolate
plain marshmallows (2)
chocolate sandwich cookies
Reese's Thins Peanut Butter Cups
plain marshmallows (2)
toffee crackers
jam (we used blueberry pomegranate)
plain marshmallows (2)
hazelnut spread
plain graham (full)
and a cherry on top

This is a monster.

It's also amazing.

Pull out the Dagwood when you truly want to impress your guests. Assembly is nearly as much fun as eating.

"I took this one home to work through over a couple of snacking sessions. It kept surprisingly well in the fridge. When I was up against a deadline and needed a sugar rush, this delivered." —Laura

THE S'MORE TEAM

JULIE BICKEL

ALENA VAN ARENDONK

LAURA VAN ARENDONK BAUGH

SUPPORT TEAM

SPARKLES THE PIT BULL—CERTIFIED DISPOSAL OF SURPLUS MARSHMALLOWS

JON BAUGH—SPREADSHEET MANAGEMENT

MARK DELLA-CROCE—SUPPLEMENTARY TESTING & TASTING TEAM

NANCY VANARENDONK—PROCESS DOCUMENTATION (VISUAL)

LARRY VANARENDONK—MORAL SUPPORT

FIND MORE AT:

LAURAVAB.COM

ALENAVANARENDONK.COM

ZJBICKEL.COM

Made in United States
North Haven, CT
16 December 2022

29253021R00058